MW01593068

Overcoming Impossible Odds:

The Steve Bottrill Story

New Dawning Press

Petrolia, Ontario, Canada

Overcoming Impossible Odds:

The Steve Bottrill Story

Steve Bottrill

Overcoming Impossible Odds:

The Steve Bottrill Story

By Steve Bottrill

Copyright 2019 Steve Bottrill

First Print Edition January 2020

ISBN: 978-1-989346-06-8

All rights reserved. No part of this book may be reproduced in any form or by electronic or mechanical means – except in the case of brief quotations embodied in articles or reviews – without written permission from the publisher.

Dedication

I dedicate this book to my incredible wife, Cathy Bottrill, my four kids Téa, Chloe, Simon, and Ben, to my amazing parents Sandra Bottrill and Geoff Bottrill (decd.) and my brother, Stuart Bottrill.

Acknowledgments

A huge thank you to my wife, Cathy Bottrill, who has been unwavering in her love. I would not be alive if it was not for her love. "Cat" stayed by my side throughout all the hardships. She has been with me day in and day out. She has given me a strength I never thought possible. I could not have done all this without her.

A big thank you to my kids, Téa, Chloe, Simon and Ben who bring a smile to my face everyday. To my parents, Geoff Bottrill (decd.) and Sandra Bottrill, who gave me everything possible. They worked hard their entire lives to give me and my brother, Stuart "Stu", every advantage. I will be forever grateful beyond words. My brother Stu, what can I say? He amazes me everyday and has always been there for me. He has a heart of gold.

My thanks to Dr. Henry Svec, without whose assistance this book would never have been written. Dr. Svec encouraged and believed in my dream of writing a book. He has been instrumental in changing my life. Dr. Svec saw something in me even when I didn't. He is revolutionary in his practice and is a visionary.

I would like to thank the writing genius of Dawn Stilwell, for sharing her knowledge and writing skills. She has been a blessing. Thank you to the author and my cousin, Samantha Bruce Benjamin, who always encouraged me to continue. Thank you to Stacey Weeks who was there for me from the start of my writing journey. She played a pivotal role in the development of this book.

To the many more people who touched my life and helped me on my journey, I thank you.

Foreword from Steve

BELIEVE and ACHIEVE

This is a book about my life and near-death experience. You will read about how I overcame the odds, how I overcame death and disability to go on to live an extraordinary life!

If you believe, you can achieve.

This book will change your life. We all have a goal or a dream that we want to accomplish; I can help you achieve it. Read how I proved the naysayers wrong and persevered. You can live an extraordinary life, regardless of your circumstances. It is possible to do what others say is impossible! I am the living proof of that! From welfare to a millionaire, from paralyzed to an aerobics instructor, from a coma to an inspiration. Read on and learn my secret to success. You, too, can rise above your circumstances and live an extraordinary life.

My purpose is to inspire you and to help you overcome *anything*.

Steve Bottrill

Contents

The Accident

My parents think I'm dead.

"You should donate his organs, before it is too late," the doctor says.

They think I can't hear them. My father's voice trembles as my mother's rises to a panicked pitch. The doctor doesn't hesitate.

"There is no hope," he says. "The ventilator is keeping him alive."

I want to laugh at how ridiculous this is. I'm fine! I wait for my dad's gruff English accent to deliver the punchline, but they continue to speak as if I'm not here.

"Mom," I try to say, but I can't make a sound. Panic rises in my chest. I try to yell, but nothing happens. I can't speak. I can't move. I can't even blink. My parents cling to each other as they nod along with the doctor.

Don't do it! The words rise internally but slam against the shell of my skin that arrests their escape. *I'm alive! I want to LIVE!*

"Even if your son does somehow survive," the doctor continues, "he will never be the same. This type of event changes a person. He'll be angry all the time. He'll wonder why this happened to him. He'll be dependent on machines and people for his entire life."

My dad's familiar brogue falls over me like a comfortable blanket.

"That's no way to live," he says. An uncomfortable silence follows. Is he actually considering this? Can't he see that I'm right here?

"We should donate his organs," he says, "and give someone else a chance at a productive life. Steve would want that."

The words hang in the thick air. *NO!* I scream. At least I try to scream, but it ricochets inside my physical trappings.

Before anyone can object, two nurses snatch me from my bed. I assume they are males by their strength and their formidable grasp on my arm and legs. One hooks me under the arms, the other by my two ankles. I'm placed on a stretcher and wheeled down the hall. A sound like I have never heard fills the corridor. A raw howl echoed off the sterile walls. It's my mom and she sounds like she is dying.

"Clear the halls! We have a donor here," someone yells. "We need to ice the organs before it's too late!"

My mother's groaning fades as the men thrust the gurney onward.

I am flopped onto an operating table, and I land with a thud, like a slab of meat placed before a butcher. Pain shoots through my upper chest. I think I broke a rib.

"Get the saw ready. There is no time to waste. Flip the body over. Let's get started. Will someone turn on my operating music?" An assertive doctor commands the room. Calm melodic opera music fills the chamber.

"Scalpel!" another authoritative voice demands.

Wait! Stop! I'm still alive! This can't be happening. This can't be real. Why won't my body move? Why can't they see that I am alive?

The doctor leans closer with his scalpel. It looks like a utility knife, the kind of blade you use for slicing boxes open, not bodies. The blade of the scalpel catches my reflection—a motionless, lifeless body. *That can't be me!*

My heart pounds like a deep bass blasting from a stereo. Why can't the doctor see my chest move?

The doctor glances toward my eyes; I swear at this moment that he can see directly into my soul, but he looks away. He doesn't see. He doesn't see a young man engaged to be married. He doesn't see a student only weeks from graduating university. He doesn't see a man who desperately, wholeheartedly, and unashamedly wants to live.

A small tear builds. It balloons until the pressure becomes too intense. I try to blink, but I can't. Why can't I blink? The droplet now bulges like a swollen waterway pressing against the boundaries of the riverbank. It creates an unbearable pressure. There is nowhere for the tear to go.

The droplet pops mercifully in a splatter out of my eyeball, slides over my upper cheekbone, and leaves a moist residue down my face. I hear the tear hit the crisp sheets underneath me. It would take a miracle for anyone to see that tear.

"Preserve the organs!"

Could it be, did he see the tear?
The doctor leans in again with an expression of determination. A sharp needle pricks my upper chest.

I black out.

Life Flashes

My mind races. I relive my life. Why am I swallowed by a thick pitch-black abyss? What's happening? Is my brain shutting down or am I still alive? Could I be somewhere in between death and life?

Flashbacks of my life race before me. I guess it is true what they say, before you die your entire life flashes before your eyes; the good things in your life, the poor choices you have made, all the random events in your life, everything. For me the flash-backs are sporadic. They are not in any particular order. The flashbacks were more than a dream. I could feel the moments in my soul, if that makes sense? I was reliving the moments in my life that formed my character. Somehow the sheer determination of overcoming barriers and proving people wrong were the strongest sense in my dreams. My entire life was about proving people wrong and becoming the best at whatever thing I set my mind to and now my best trait was going to shine. *I AM GOING TO PROVE THEM WRONG.*

When I was around five years of age, our family moved to a new street from across town. The name of the street was Chestnut Drive. It was located more toward the east end of town, the rougher part of Chatham. Our neighbourhood was separated from the east end by a busy road called Park Ave. to the north and another street called Park Lane to the south. The entire area I grew up in was surrounded by kids. Not just any type of kids; they were rough and tough kids. We never wanted to stray too far from our own subdivision for fear we would bump into some of these tough kids, which had happened on a few occasions. There were always stories of fights and rough-housing whenever someone bumped into one of the kids from the surrounding streets. I was never seen as a tough guy, but I could hold my own, I think. I was always too 'chicken' to confront an 'East Ender'. We had been caught a few times when going to the variety store down the street, called Charlie's Variety.

I can remember one time when my younger brother saw a darker skinned boy. My brother could not have been more than 6 years old at the time. He saw a dark-skinned boy and called him a rude name. Next thing you know, we were encircled by 8 kids who were a few years older. My brother had a giant gobstopper in his mouth. You could see it popping out of his little cheek. The younger and much bigger dark-skinned boy wound up and punched my brother in the side of the mouth, directly where the gob-stopper was in his mouth. It was quick thinking on my brother's part; he moved the gobstopper over to the other side of his mouth. Funnily enough, once we changed schools from the catholic elementary school to the public elementary right next door to that, my brother and that same kid became best friends. We were just little kids and didn't really know what was going on.

After the variety store incident, the circle of kids broke up and everyone went their separate ways. My brother and I walked home. It was a silent walk, until my brother said, "It's a good thing I moved my gobstopper."

We really didn't know what to think. We were both relieved to still be walking and not to have been beated up too badly. We just knew we liked candy and would continue our daily commute to Charlie's Variety.

In my neighbourhood, kids would call other kids insulting names and ask to fight but nothing ever happened, as long as we looked tough and had a tough guy walk, we were usually fine. We had to learn the 'lingo' of the street fairly quickly to survive in such a rough and tough area.

The kids in the area were a mixture of all ages and ethnicities. As long as you played sports, you were included into the cool group. I quickly learned how to play sports like road hockey, baseball and soccer. We would play in the big double crescent that was Chestnut Drive. There were kids older than myself and kids that were younger. All the kids in my street were excellent athletes. They all excelled at their own schools and even beyond at the county level. I had to learn to compete at a high level at everything. We would play a game called 'The game of the game of the game'. The idea of the game was: the big kids, which there were two, would team up and chase the younger kids, which there were about 10. The goal of the game was to capture all the younger kids and put them in jail, usually a porch. The only way a captured kid could be rescued was by someone on his own team tagging him out of jail, without the rescuing kid getting taken down himself. In order to put a kid in jail, the older kids would have to wrestle you to the ground. Everything and every game was a competition.

After my fifth year at my elementary school, we switched schools for one reason or another. The new public elementary school was right next to the catholic elementary school I had first attended. Once we did change schools, the toughness and fighting really escalated. For some reason, the kids there thought I was a tough kid, perhaps because I was good at sports, or maybe because I had the tough guy walk and talk. My best friend also went to the same public elementary school, and had been there since kindergarten. The difference was, however, the other kids didn't see him as a tough guy. Having repeated grade five, I was determined to show everyone I was smart. School subjects seemed easy for me at the new school. It was a fresh start, plus I was in the same classroom as my best friend and we would always compete at everything. I hated losing and being seen as slower, weaker or not as smart. I had to win and beat him at everything. Fortunately enough, he and I were always the best in the class at sports and academics. We competed at everything. I was only really a few months older than he was. (My birthday is Christmas Eve and his was some time in the summer). Repeating the fifth grade was the best thing for me. It really built my self-confidence and my drive to compete. I was really small for my age so I fit right in with my peers. Not wanting to lose was a pride thing as well. I knew I was a bit older than everyone else, and technically I should not lose. I wanted to win at everything.

There were two kids who prided themselves in having a killer headlock. Once they snuck up behind you and locked their arms around your neck, it was lights out, fight is over. Good thing I could hold my breath for a long time. We had a pool growing up which came in handy for moments like the headlock.

After only 2 years at this public school, my parents decided to move houses. The area was getting rougher and rougher by the day. My old friends had all started to move away about that time as well. The street was not the same. My parents decided to move across town to a new subdivision. Lo and behold, I was to start at a new school and this time, without any friends. That was hard going because once again I had to prove myself because I was so much smaller than everyone at my new school. I was going from a school with predominantly kids from my area to now kids from the country. All the kids seemed so big and strong now. I was still tiny. I was an easy target for bigger kids. I was shy and quiet and not willing to fight back too often. I was still good at certain sports though. But no longer did I excel at everything. I was just a 'good' player. These country kids were big and strong. I still had the drive but it was harder to be one of the best athletes. Some kids were six feet tall while I was still only four feet tall.

High School Begins & Life Changes, Again

After grade eight I went to high school. The school was a 15-minute walk down the street from my house. The high school I was now attending was seen as a sports school, not necessarily academic. In order to be a popular person at this school, you had to be a sports hero. I went there in grade nine and was only four feet nothing and sixty pounds. I was small. I can remember looking up to the 'jocks' of the day and thinking, *man, they are so popular and well-liked and get all the girls. That is what I want to be like one day.* Instead for now, I was seen as an awkward little kid with no athletic prowess, or personality. I was always bullied and seen as a loner. I didn't have many friends, due to switching schools and being shy and quiet. Whenever someone would pick on me, I would think, *one day I will be the best athlete and strongest person in school and get the most popular girl. I will be the ONE. I would keep a strong mind and all the girls will all fall in love with me. I will be the one that everyone envies.*

The only way to be the best athlete was to take all the Phys. Ed classes every year and compete against the best. That is what I did. I took Phys. Ed class every year. Even though I was small when I first started high school, I tried my hardest to be the best athlete and beat everyone. That tenacity served me well for my life's work of becoming the best at every sport and everything I tried. Needless to say, I finally hit my growth spurt around grade eleven and grade twelve. I was years behind everyone else physically but my mind set seemed to surpass everyone, because I would never give up no matter how dire the circumstances. I always believed that one day I was going to be the best and most popular and I would not stop until I achieved my goal. Others had already given up and I was just getting started! I started to excel at sports again, becoming one of the fastest runners at my school and achieving remarkable success in soccer. I even started to date one of the most popular girls at our high school. I had accomplished my goal of becoming a 'stable topper'.

Myself and my best friend at the time in high school had developed a societal paradigm, and a diagram of how we saw high school. It was like a pyramid.

As we go from the top down to the bottom of the pyramid (the paradigm of high school) there are more and more people. At the top are the stable toppers. Here are the people who are the best at everything - sports, academics, good-looking, popular, and most of all they are the good people who everyone wants to be around. They talk to everyone no matter their status in life or their status in school. And they don't see themselves as a popular or amazing. A stable topper would never tell people they are a stable topper and never see themselves as a stable topper.

The false toppers are the next level down. They are the people who think they are stable toppers but they don't talk to everyone and anyone, depending on their status in life or at school. False toppers are usually mean-spirited and make fun of others whom they feel are less than themselves. False toppers will never be envied or idolized but mistakenly think other people idolize them.

Mid-graders are the mid-level group. These are the type of people who are happy where they are and they have no ambition. They barely scrape by. They are the group that doesn't particularly want to do anything special in life.

Last are the bottom feeders. This group consists of all the smokers and drug dealers and people that dress with the tough guy leather jackets with a gang symbol. There seemed to always be a lot of smokers and guys and girls that thought they were the tough guys. They always got into fights. At my school we had a Jr B hockey team, the Chatham Maroons. It was always the bottom feeders against the Maroons. They always seemed to scrap one another. The bottom feeders were always worried about being cool, about what sort of trouble they can get into and their reputation of being misfits.

Floaters are the people that don't fit into any group but fit in anywhere. Floaters are friendly and they get along with everyone. They just float through life without a care. Stable toppers would characterize themselves as floaters. A floater is no one special. A floater is the cloud in the side of the pyramid. The cloud goes up and down.

Climbers are a group of people who are trying to raise their own status and will try their hardest to become somebody important. You can see spurts of greatness from them. Their popularity goes up and down. Climbers tend to only associate with stable toppers and false toppers. The climber location on the pyramid is on the side wall trying to get to the top.

It is the stable toppers who always seemed to be the popular kids and they always had a girlfriend. And not just any type of girls; they were the prettiest and most beautiful of all the girls. The stable toppers were the ones my friend and I looked up to. I wanted to be a stable topper. The trouble was that all the stable toppers stuck together. I knew I could become a stable topper. One day, I would be the popular kid with all the glory and the girls, looked up to by others.

The best way for me to become a stable topper was to become good at sports again and have my name on the morning announcements. When you constantly have your name on the announcements at my high school, people start to talk about you. Every morning the school secretary would read off the daily announcements; what was happening in the school with the different groups and teams and who was scoring goals and who were the outstanding athletes for the day. Getting my name on the morning announcements was essentially a way for me to become a stable topper. I had a goal and a dream. There was a direction for my life. You must believe! Believe in yourself even when no one else does.

I would concentrate on playing soccer and badminton. My dad was my travel soccer coach when I was a young kid, and he was a very good one at that. One of the best in Canada. My dad is from England and grew up with soccer in his blood, very knowledgeable. He was actually one of the three men that started a soccer league in Chatham and surrounding area. I also concentrated on playing badminton because we always played it when my family went up north to a cottage for the summer. I had just played badminton with my friends a few days earlier at the YMCA before we started to play in grade 9 Phys. Ed. class.

I was always a good athlete but I was half the size of the other kids. I was quiet and shy but I hoped my ability would shine. That didn't happen, no one took any notice of me. I was seen as an easy person to cut from the team tryouts. I somewhat suspect that my personality might have had something to do with that. I was one of those nice guys. During my Phys. Ed. classes and at the team tryouts, I would partner up with whoever asked me first, and it wasn't the popular and most athletic guys. It was always the quiet and non-athletic person. Consequently, I seemed like I was not athletic. I can remember during the badminton tryouts my grade 10 year; we would play against an opponent and the winner would then write the score down on a sheet. Of course, I won every game but I didn't write the score down, my opponent did. I was being nice and let my opponent write the score. I trusted my opponent to write the correct score. But, of course, they wrote the opposite and as a result, I did not make the team. A team where I clearly was the best player.

That year, my Phys. Ed. teacher was the badminton coach. He had been the badminton coach since he had started teaching at the high school. We had some players from the badminton team in our Phys. Ed. class. My teacher liked to play badminton during the class. During a couple of weeks, the teacher had set up a class badminton tournament. The teacher fully expected his players to win the class tournament. But seemingly out of nowhere, *I* won. I mean, I knew I was going to win. I was short and quiet and shy but I was determined and had a drive to prove myself. I never bragged or was full of myself. I just needed a chance. If no one was going to give me a chance or the opportunity, I would make one. In my life, it always seemed like I needed to prove myself. My Phys. Ed teacher was coaching the badminton team the following year and he asked me to play for him. He also asked me, "Why didn't you try out for the team last year?"

I said, "I did!"

I was starting to prove myself at school. Now, not only had the kids started to see my abilities but the coaches had started to see as well. My confidence was starting to blossom. The next step? Getting my name on the morning announcements for winning an event. I was going from shy and quiet to confident and more outgoing. I was still intimidated by the false toppers, but I was growing and getting stronger. I was going to be a stable topper! I was going to achieve the high school dream. I never gave up; I was going to prove them all wrong. A motto that would stick with me my entire life.

It's funny because many years later, I would find out those same stable toppers were not stable toppers at all, they were really false toppers and had been taking steroids. After high school, those so-called stable toppers did not achieve anything at all. They had dead-end jobs and became fat and out of shape. No one looked up to them in the real world. I still see those pretend stable toppers from high school to this day, and it is funny because they still talk about high school days. But now, they exaggerate or even make things up about their high school career.

I would continue to try out for school teams like soccer and badminton. I knew I could make those two teams. If only I could make it onto a team, I could make my name.

Grade 11 rolled around with much promise. I had the opportunity within my grasp to make the badminton team this year. My confidence was starting to develop. I was working part-time at this point in my life at a department store called Woolco, the predecessor to Walmart. I started to work there because my mother was working there. I had to start coming out of my shell and talk to customers and staff. At this point in my life, I felt Woolco was exactly what I needed. They had sports teams at Woolco. Teams like baseball, although I was not chosen to play on that team. What a letdown. Oh well, I will prove them wrong. I will be the best!

The next practice the team had, I went because I had nothing else to do. I went to the practice and did very well. I won a game of '21'. I caught a ball within the crowd of people. It meant a lot to me to prove them wrong. To prove they had made a mistake by not choosing me to play in the tournament.

Unfortunately, soccer tryouts were at the same time as badminton at my high school. I tried out for both soccer and badminton. I did not end up making the soccer team. There were some phenomenal kids that came to my high school to play soccer that year, some of the best players in town. They were trying to make the all-Ontario competition that year. I don't believe they advanced that far.

My confidence continued to grow and I was being talked to by some of the girls. I even went on a date! That was a really big deal to me. I did not ask the girl. She asked me.

Grades OAC (12 & 13): The Journey Begins

I was really starting to grow into myself now. This was the year some of my old Taekwondo friends were travelling to Spain for a tournament. I told my friends, "I am going to make a comeback. I want to go to Spain."

I had already achieved a black belt years ago and was at one time an accomplished fighter. I was pretty good back when I was a teenager. I called up the Taekwondo school and decided to give it a try. I went back to sparring, competition style. I had lost a lot of speed, was taller and it was a bit odd fighting again, but I did ok. I ended upgoing to Spain. That was a trip of a lifetime. However, I lost my first two fights.

There was a shift in my life at this time. Kids at school started to take notice of me. I was becoming more popular. My goal of becoming a stable topper had been met. I used to walk around the school halls avoiding eye contact, always with my head down. Now, after associating with some stable toppers and having the most stable topper girlfriend of everyone, I walked around with my head up and talked to everyone. I had done it. The teachers and staff would talk to me. The cafeteria ladies were talking to me now. What a difference! I would walk into the cafeteria and everyone would want to be around me and chat with me. I had done it! I thought, *this is what it feels like to have a girlfriend and be popular, to be a stable topper. Life's good. Let's keep this feeling alive. I want this feeling my entire life, I will have this feeling my entire life. Life awaits. Let's conquer.*

If there is one important lesson I learned from my high school days, it is that if you can see it, you can believe it, and you can achieve it!

University

Now I was off to university for another challenge. I needed to live by myself, without my parents. I was in a strange city, far away. There was no turning back. I did not have a car anyway, and it was a good eight-hour drive back to Chatham. I did not know anyone and had to prove myself again.

My first challenge was making the soccer team. It was a different type of motivation; it was more of an internal motivation. I was no longer concerned about becoming a stable topper. My motivation and drive would have to come from inside myself.

Soccer season would begin at the start of the school year. Tryouts started before school had even begun. I was out of 'soccer shape' because I had not played that summer back in Chatham. I gave the tryouts my best effort. I had never been around such amazing soccer players. There were players on the team who were professionals and even players who were on the Olympic team! All of the players were in great shape. I managed to stick around for the first set of cuts but there would still be a second round of cuts before the final team was selected. I was part of the second group that was cut from the team. What a disappointment. I was a star in high school and now I was off the university team, knocked down from the pyramid. I would have to climb again.

I still had a bit of confidence left within because of the best-looking girl from my Frosh group (a group that first year kids are put into before the school year begins. It is used to help introduce one another and to get to know the school. It is a real party atmosphere). There was a girl who was in second year that was our leader, who was interested in me. All the guys wanted to be with her, but I got her number and was always talking to her. I even had a few shopping dates with her. I used the line, "Since I don't know Ottawa very well and may need help, can I get your phone number?" I can't believe that line worked on her!

Once soccer season started, I went to watch a couple games, but I had to pay money to watch and so I could only afford to watch a couple of games. I sat high in the bleachers so I would not be seen. The team was ranked number two in the country. They were a very skillful team. If I wanted to make this team next year, I would really have to develop my skills.

I had a new goal to reach for and felt I needed to achieve my goal. My life had a purpose. It was a goal that seemed out of reach, but I knew I could achieve it with determination and dedication. I believed in myself. At this point, I was not content with myself and my current status in life. I felt like I was 'a mid-grader' or at least a 'climber'. I was driven to achieve greatness. I had to become a 'stable topper' in life. I did not want to just be another kid who was cut from the team. I HAD to be more. I had to push myself to be great. I had to take action. I HAD TO BE A STABLE TOPPER.

I heard the soccer team was practicing indoors during the winter. I went to my first practice and was absolutely nervous. Here I was, a strange kid coming to play with a great team that was already well established. I must have done ok because I was invited back to the players' dressing room. From that point on, I felt like I was part of the team. I could not believe it; they had their own dressing room with showers and all the amenities. I kept this routine for a few weeks, getting up early, practicing in the morning with the team and at night, running the stairs in my apartment building. I lived on the 19th floor of an apartment building in Ottawa, so there were plenty of stairs and ways to keep in shape with a little ingenuity. I was dedicated to my cause. In the basement of my building were racquetball courts. Every day, I would take a soccer ball down to the courts and practice playing soccer. I was determined to make the team, to become a great again, to get that feeling back of being a stable topper. After a month of my practice routine, playing soccer with the university team in the morning, practicing at night in my apartment and also playing for a team in Ottawa on the weekends, I was really starting to improve. The coach from Carleton asked me to play on his team next year. I was so excited that as soon as I returned to my apartment, I called my dad back in Chatham. I continued playing a bit of soccer with the Ottawa team over the next month on the weekends.

I had a difficult time finding a part-time job in Ottawa and so I had to return to Chatham for the summer. The soccer teams in the Chatham area were already picked for the season and I ended up playing on a garbage team in a different city, about an hour away.

Around the same time, I met a girl named Cat and over the next year, we dated then got engaged. I had to return to Ottawa over the next couple years to finish my schooling. It was tough on our relationship to live so far away in Ottawa but I would visit when I could. Since we were engaged, Cat was enthusiastically making wedding plans. I needed to return home to help out with my own wedding. The cost for the train or the bus was expensive, though. I needed to find another way to get home.

The Drives Home Begin

One day, I was walking through the halls of Carleton University, more of a common area near a restaurant/bar area and out of curiosity, I looked at one of the many bulletin boards on the wall. It was a board that displayed posters of different items for sale or purchase. The section of the board I was interested in was the section that offered rides to different cities. In the middle of this board, written on a page, was the advertisement from a person offering a ride back and forth to Chatham, Ontario. The ride would only cost $20. Call: 613-555-5555. Leaving for Chatham every two weeks. Please call Gay.

I could not believe my eyes. Was this possible? This person was going back to my hometown that no one in Ottawa even knew existed and at an affordable price. A train ticket cost $200 and the bus, $100. There must be a 'catch'! *Oh well, let's call this person named Gay and find out.* I immediately ripped off a strip of the dangling perforated paper with the phone number on it.

I called the number as soon as I returned to my apartment. I was waiting for the 'catch', but found that there wasn't one. I discovered that Gay worked for the RCMP in Ottawa. She was a single lady and visited her boyfriend in Chatham every two weeks. She travelled with her big dog in the back seat and just wanted someone to keep her company. From that point on, I had a ride home every two weeks. Gay mentioned she never travelled during inclement weather. I was also in agreement, as I thought that was a wise decision.

Every two weeks for the majority of the school year, we would travel back and forth to Chatham. However, there were times due to the unfavourable weather conditions that we did not make the trip. Two of the most notable times we did not travel occurred during the months of February and the beginning of March.

The end of March was upon us and the weather was starting to clear. Neither myself nor Gay had been to Chatham for a good month. We were both anxious and excited to get back to Chatham. We both had our own reasons for the visit.

I had a phone conversation with Gay the night before and we made plans to return to Chatham the next day. Gay would arrive at my house at 5:00 am and if all went well, we would drive the eight or nine-hour ride back to Chatham and be home in time for supper.

I was one of five students who rented this particular house in Ottawa. I rented the house with my best friend, Jason, and two other girls. The girls were very annoying, to be honest with you. I always enjoyed going home because not only did I have the opportunity to see Cat, but my dad would give me $50 for the weekend. Another amenity I enjoyed when going home was driving. In Ottawa, I was taking the bus everywhere. Now there was an interesting way to travel. I had bought a yearly bus pass but, on most occasions, I would walk to my destinations. During my walks, nine out of ten times I would help push a car out of snow. There was an incredible amount of snowfall in Ottawa. Whenever I pushed someone out of snow, the driver would say, "God bless you!" That always felt nice. The blessings sure would come in handy later on in life.

The first time I rode the bus was a real eye-opener. I heard many people speaking French and English and interchanging the languages. I never knew there were that many French speakers around. There was only a few people that I knew of back in Chatham that spoke French. I guess I was really naive. I never paid attention during my French classes at school because I had no interest. Now I was engaged to a French girl and was living in a bilingual city. Talk about irony.

The plans were in place for Gay to arrive at my house at 5:00 am on March 22, 1996. I had been on the phone with Cat the night before and we had made big plans for the weekend. We were both excited. It seemed like a lifetime since I had been home.

After ending my phone conversation with Cat, I continued to pack my belongings for the weekend. The weather was clear and all seemed right on schedule. I had set my alarm for 5:00 am to grab a quick toast from the kitchen and be on my way. I would only pack a gym bag with one change of clothes, a few snacks, and my cassette Walkman. I had recorded a bunch of my favourite songs on a cassette tape. Usually the songs were 'Top 40' songs of the day. I always liked to listen to my Walkman on the drive home, recline my seat as much as I could while trying to avoid the big dog in the back seat and fall asleep. I must not have been good company for Gay. I was a shy, quiet kind of guy.

I didn't drink much alcohol at the time and wasn't much for approaching strangers I didn't know. The only time I decided to speak to someone out of the blue was when I needed something. One day, I was riding my bicycle through the school campus and I heard someone playing guitar. It was a nice, pleasant type of music, almost like a folk song. I followed the sound to see two guys were playing guitar. It looked to me like the guy with long hair was a rock star and was teaching the younger guy. I rode my bike over and listened for a bit until they stopped and looked my way with a puzzled look. I told them, "Sounds really good. Do you give lessons? I am really interested in playing guitar and do not have a lot of money to go to a music store and I don't know Ottawa very well."

The rock star, who was dressed in typical grunge rock star musician clothes, answered, "I am teaching my friend". Then he agreed to teach me guitar and we exchanged numbers. He would come to my house once a week and teach me guitar. After a short period of time our friendship changed. He was older than me and seemed to me more 'worldly'. He was telling me about Jack Kerouac and his book 'On the Road'. I immediately went to the library and read the book. I was hooked. I started to research the Beat Writers. If I wasn't in class, I could be found at the library reading the Beat Writers. I read a lot of poetry and short stories over the next year by Allen Ginsberg, William Burroughs and others. I always had a book in my hand. I wasn't a reader before, but now I was fully invested in reading and writing.

On another occasion, my guitar teacher/friend brought over a 6 pack of Busch beer. It tasted like no other beer I drank. It had a foamy taste, very unique. Again, I was hooked, I now had a beer I enjoyed.

The morning of March 22 began with a loud buzz from my alarm clock. I had set the old digital clock to buzz because the radio did not work. The radio clock was over ten years old. I was too cheap to buy a new one and I needed all the money I could get my hands on. Why buy a new clock when this one was working fine? I was getting quick at jumping out of bed and turning the alarm off so not to wake the rest of the house. I was so good that as soon as I heard the alarm clock engage, I was up out of bed before the alarm fully sounded. The buzzer from the alarm clock was extremely loud and would wake the entire house if I left it to buzz for a long period of time. The alarm clock was a step away from my bed, resting on an old cardboard box I had used to pack my belongings from the move a year earlier. I intentionally placed the alarm clock far enough away so that I would have to get out of bed to turn it off. It was a strategy I used to get myself out of bed and not miss class. My strategy did not always work out. I enjoyed the smallest room in the house because it seemed like I had the last "dibs" and I was the last one informed about the house.

I was up out of bed, looking forward to a great weekend at home. I did not enjoy the travel so much, but it was a necessary evil. I quickly threw on a pair of jeans and grabbed my gym bag off the floor that I had prepared the night before. I reached behind me to put on my necklace. It was a wooden old cross with brown leather string that Cat had given me to wear for extra protection. I wasn't a big believer in that sort of thing but I wore it for Cat and plus it was a reminder of her.

I ran down the first set of five steps to the bathroom. We had two bathrooms in the house, one for Jason and I that was halfway up the house on a small floor and the other one was for the girls. The girls' bathroom happened to be directly across the hall from my bedroom on the top floor. The boys' bathroom was much smaller was located five steps down a set of stairs. The boys' bathroom was just a basic shower stall, sink and toilet and was not decorated at all. Meanwhile, in the girls' bathroom, they had decorated it to the max; pinks and plush everywhere, teddy bears, and flowers. To me, why bother decorating a bathroom? It was a bathroom. I just need a toilet, somewhere to do my business.

I ran into the bathroom, ready to start a full day of travel. I brushed my teeth then packed up my toothbrush into my gym bag, washed my face and took a leak. I knew it was going to be a long drive and I should be prepared not to stop for a while.

I made my way down the next set of 6 stairs to the kitchen on the main floor. Our house was a split level; the bedrooms were located up the 'L' shaped stairs and a kitchen, living room, and dining room were on the main floor. Downstairs was our laundry room, and the remainder of the basement was Jason's bedroom. There was an outside door in the basement as well.

I placed by gym bag on the floor next to the front door. I did not bother to look out the front door as I was in too much of a rush. I jogged to the kitchen and grabbed a slice of bread from the fridge. We had divided up the fridge into different sections. My designated shelf was the middle of the fridge. The smallest and most awkward spot in the fridge, the section where all the food is jammed into in order for it to fit, destroying the food in the process. I didn't keep much food in the fridge anyway, just the essentials. I put my bread in our toaster and pushed the lever down. The toaster was supposed to be stainless steel but it was covered with dirt and grime so it was impossible to see the stainless steel. It was stained from the moment we had brought it home. The toaster was one of those garage sales buys. The toast popped up. I buttered the toast. I used Jason's butter because I was too cheap to buy my own butter. Jason bought the real butter not that fake margarine. I launched the butter knife into the sink for someone else to clean and off I went to the front door.

I walked to the front door with half the toast still hanging out of my mouth. I slipped my fake look-alike red Doc Martin shoes on. I did not tie the shoes up because it made them easier to slip on and off. The shoes were stretched out enough to feel comfortable. I grabbed my big leather winter coat off the banister, slung my arms into the arm holes and shrugged the coat around my shoulders. I would take it off shortly after being in the car so I did not bother buttoning it up. I looked outside for Gay. She wasn't there but something else was. We were hit by a surprise snowstorm in the middle of the night. It was too late to change our minds now. There was no way to communicate with her at this point. She had not called me and I did not want to bother calling her. The plans were already set. Gay was late but it was understandable considering the weather conditions. There must have been a good 2-3 feet of snow out there.

Five minutes had passed before I looked outside again. I had kept myself busy by rummaging through my gym bag to ensure I had a change of clothes and an extra pair of socks I was sure I would need if the snow soaked through my shoes as I walked to Gay's car. There was no need for boots I thought, since the weather in Chatham was beautiful the last I had heard. Boots would take up extra space, which was a valuable commodity in a small compact car.

I looked outside again and there was Gay parked on the side of the road with her four-way flashers on, waiting for me. The roads looked a complete mess; the snowplows had not been out yet and a fresh white blanket of snow was glistening off the road.

I went out the front door as quietly as possible, so as not to wake anyone. In front of me was fresh snow and there were no footprints in the snow for me to step on to avoid having a soaker. It was going to be no fun riding an eight-hour car ride with a soaker, as there was nowhere for me to dry my feet. The car was small and it was tight quarters. I dared to step out into the snow, stepping quickly but lightly. I shut the door behind me. Next, I would have to traverse my way across the fluffy light snow to the road where Gay was parked waiting for me. Growing up in Canada, I had learned a technique to bound across the snow without sinking too deeply into the fluffy white stuff.

Gay's car was only a few feet away, but the biggest obstacle was still awaiting me, Gay was idling her car up against a large snowbank. I had to climb over the snowbank in order to enter her car and I was determined to keep my feet dry. I had made it to the embankment without too much snow seeping into my shoe. I took my first step onto the side of the snow hill with my gym bag over my shoulder that added more weight to my thin frame. The next step was going to be crucial. The next step could make or break the entire trip. I need to shift my weight as gently as possible without placing too much weight onto my stationary leg. As I attempt to lunge for the car, I could hear the snow beneath me crackle. Before I sunk knee high into the snow, I made a motion toward the car door. I had done it! I was over the mountain of snow and in the car safely. No soaker for me. I didn't bother putting my bag into the back seat. Instead, I just whipped it inside the car with me. It was going to be a comfortable trip. My stomach started to get a nervous and excited feeling; I was finally going home. With all the snow ahead of us, I was sure it would be a treacherous trip.

We set off and once on the highway, I felt a bit of relief. I was reaching for my Walkman to listen to some tunes when the unthinkable happened. A car coming toward us in the opposite lane lost control and spun out. Gay yanked the steering wheel left and then right. We were in a fish tail and the car seemed out of control. We were skidding on the snow and ice. Thankfully, Gay managed to steer us to safety.

Just a little wakeup call, that's all, I thought to myself. We had narrowly avoided a catastrophe. The severity of the moment had not set in for a few minutes. We were silent until Gay asked, "Do you want to continue?"

I told her, "It's up to you."

Maybe it would be ok? Surely, that would not happen again. Secretly though, I was hoping she would turn around. However, we continued on our return trip to Chatham. I placed my headphones back over my ears, reclined my seat and fell asleep. Gay woke me once we reached the St. Thomas McDonald's service station. I was starving! Once I awoke and regained my senses, I checked the time. It was already 5:00 pm. We had been traveling for twelve hours. Gay said the drive was extremely slow and she was being cautious because of the snowstorm. We had been travelling the 401 West, the main highway that stretches the full length of Ontario. It is the busiest highway in North America. The actual speed limit is 100km per hour but we had been driving at around 60 km per hour the entire trip, hence the extra- long drive.

Once at the McDonald's, I ordered my usual McChicken combo. Gay ordered a Big Mac combo and an extra cheeseburger for her dog in the back seat. We were only about an hour away from Chatham now, at usual driving speeds. Maybe at this rate, we would be another two hours to Chatham. I finished my McChicken combo and I told Gay to wake me when we were home, which was unusual for me. It is funny because there was only a short distance to Chatham and I would usually stay awake for the remainder of the trip. I thought I would wake from the sudden slowing of the car off of the highway. I couldn't recline my seat too much because there was a big dog in the back seat. I would just have to make the best of my uncomfortable position. So, that's what I did, and I fell back to sleep. That's the last thing I remember before waking up in the hospital after the accident.

My Life Changes Forever

The next thing I knew, I could hear a stranger talking to my parents. I still had my eyes closed and thought maybe it was a dream.

"When and if Steve wakes, he will never be the same. He may not remember you. He will never play sports again or go to school again. He may not walk again or ever be the same person. He will never be 100% again. Steve has sustained a massive brain injury and internal injuries. His spleen has been damaged, his liver damaged, he has a deflated lung, his hips are damaged, he is blind. To be honest with you ma'am, only one in a million make it back to leading a normal independent life. Seriously, you should think about donating Steve's organs. We need you to answer that question quickly because we don't have much time before his organs shut down for good." the doctor explained to my mother.

In my mind I was thinking, *of course I will remember my parents and my fiancé. What the heck is going on? Who is this strange voice I can hear? I will prove them wrong. I will be better than 100%.*

Someone or something flipped a switch in my brain in that moment. I had determination like never before. I had a sudden surge and strength throughout my body. I don't know how or why I heard this conversation or where I gathered the strength and fortitude to persevere and an outright will to defy the odds and the so-called experts, but I was going to prove them wrong. I decided then and there that nothing was going to stop me!

I had many visitors in those first days at the hospital. I could tell you exactly where those people were sitting in my room just from the sounds of their voices. My fiancé came to visit me every day and it was her belief in me that gave me the extra love and strength to persevere. My parents and brother would often come to visit which helped to give me the added push when I needed. Later, I would also hear about all the prayers many thousands of people had sent my way.

At one point, while on my supposed death bed, a priest had come to read my final rites and the strangest thing happened. I can still feel this experience. Father Mike Dwyer, a priest my fiancé had known for years, came into my room and was going to read my last rites. He took his time and made conversation with everyone in my room before he stepped to my bedside to proceed. Out of his upper pocket, he pulled a very special cross. The cross was made of some type of metal. He started off the ceremony by saying some prayers and giving thanks for my life. He placed the metal cross on my forehead and suddenly, something strange began to happen. The hospital instruments and all the machines I was connected to started to sound and react to the cross. Father Mike removed the cross and all the machines and devices returned to their original state. He placed the cross back onto my forehead and once again the machines and instruments went bizarre with sounds. It was like a powerful, unexplained phenomenon.

After this, Father Mike told my fiancé, "Steve will be fine. In fact, he will do great things with his life."

Exhausted from the visit, Father Mike Dwyer excused himself, telling Cat, "I have to get back to my church." Cat thanked him, and Father Mike exited without concluding the final rites ceremony.

A Day Later, Out of The Coma

My eyes open. I must be alive! The doctor must have seen the tear, I think to myself. I awaken with two strange gentlemen standing at the end of my bed. They are identical twins dressed in the same exact clothing. They are wearing nice, crisp, clean hospital scrubs. The two of them move in unison. *Wait a second*, I think to myself, *is it the same person? Yes, it is.* I must be waking up and my eyes have not adjusted and focused yet.

"Do you know what happened to you?" he asks. I cannot seem to form a response, so the man continues.

"You were asleep in the passenger seat of a car that hit a patch of ice and went into an uncontrollable spin. A car coming the opposite direction must have hit the same ice and t-boned your car directly where you were sitting. It was the most horrific car accident ever. You were crushed. The car you were in was destroyed. No one knows how you survived. The paramedics had to revive your heart many times. The body bag was ready. You were rushed to the Chatham hospital, they couldn't do much for you, and then you were rushed here to London. There is not much hope for you."

"What...?" my mouth moved but no sounds came out.

The male nurse continued, "You have been in a coma for ten days. You can't talk because there is a trach in your throat which is keeping you alive. And you are connected to all of these instruments and machines. We had to strap you to the bed because you had tried to get up. You fell off the end of the bed when you tried to walk. You have no muscle strength in your legs and you collapsed. You have a feeding tube stapled onto your body because you ripped the last one out when it was taped to your body. You are extremely lucky to be alive. Your third and fourth vertebrae were badly bruised. If they had broken, you would have died instantly. Your internal organs were a mess and we had to open up your rib cage and do an emergency operation. You had a one percent chance of survival. No one, including the doctors, thought you were going to make it.

"Do you realize your journey? You were first at Victoria hospital and your parents, family and fiancé had come to see you because no one thought you would survive the night. Then, you were not expected to make it to the next day and definitely not a week or even two. But you survived. You are holding on to something. You have a big purpose, my friend. Everyone is just happy you are alive. We are told just to make you comfortable. We have been told to do what we can to make you comfortable but don't expect miracles. The doctor noticed at the last second, and I mean last second that you were still alive. We had the gurney ready and everything to transport your organs for donation. Holy, did Dr. Mann ever lambast those nurses who put you on the surgical table! I have never seen him so mad before. He is usually a calm specimen. We won't be seeing those nurses around here anymore," he said with a chuckle. "Oh, and by the way it's April 2, 1996. With that being said, he walked out.

You must have the wrong guy; I can stand up and walk out of here right now.

My mouth moved but no sounds came out. I tried to move but I was tied to the bed. I pulled and yanked on the tethers. It was no use; I was well restrained. Weary, I fall back asleep.

It was all beginning to make sense. Those conversations I had heard earlier about donating my organs, about never being the same, about being mad all the time; it was not a dream. The surge of energy, strength and determination was not for nothing. Maybe the male nurse is right? My ribs are itchy from the stitch marks that wrap around my side and my back is sore. I have double vision from the injuries to my eyes. Heck, I can barely see. I can't move my eyes. Nothing worse than being blind, I thought. I also have some sort of strange metal contraption attached to my head. I can feel the weight of it on my shoulders. I know it is metal because when I touch it with my head when I tip my head side to side, it feels cold, solid and smooth. It feels like a giant building on top of my shoulders.

Therapy Begins

I awoke, not sure of anything. Therapy of various types start immediately. The therapy sessions of physiotherapy, occupational therapy, speech therapy, and recreational therapy are located in the basement of the hospital and my room is located on the fifth floor. A porter comes to my room to push me in my wheelchair to the different therapy rooms.

It is so annoying; the porter always takes so long to come for me. I have a look of disapproval on my face. I hope she is aware of my face. She certainly does take a long time. The porter is a petite Asian woman. When I finally arrive at therapy, I am so tired from the wait that I fall back to sleep. That was a waste. I was so eager to begin the process but the ride from the fifth floor to the basement was too much stimulation on my still healing brain.

"I can't believe this. Steve will never get any better, he just falls asleep. How can we do any sort of rehab with him when he falls asleep? I guess we are getting paid anyway.", one of the male physio-therapists chuckles. What he said annoyed me.

That's it! I thought to myself. *More determined than ever, I will show them!*

No one thinks I can hear, but I certainly can. I have to relearn how to do most everything, from going to the bathroom myself, (you know going number two and cleaning yourself afterward), to eating by myself using utensils and not using a feeding tube, learning how to use a cup again without the sippy safeguard, showering myself, you name it, I have to relearn it. *But I will show them!* I will amaze them with my recovery. No one will ever laugh at me again.

A Month has Passed

I have been at this same hospital for a month now and the rooms are starting to feel suffocating. I am starting to move my limbs more freely and with purpose. No longer do I feel like a lump of coal. It has been a long time and I have a sense of urgency to go home. I can finally take showers without assistance (I always felt uneasy with someone soaping me down and watching me and giving me instructions in the shower, especially about washing my privates. I am glad that is behind me). The feeding tube is gone, I can eat food all by myself now, and I have relearned how to use utensils. I can walk without using a walker now. Life is looking up.

On my way to the showers, I have to pass the nurses station. Every morning, it was the same conversation.

"Hi Steve, how are you?"

"I am doing great!"

I would always say "great", even if I was not feeling well. I never let my negative side out, always trying to stay positive. I just want to get out of the hospital and go home. If I could fool the nurses and everyone else in the hospital then maybe I could go home earlier. I am walking with purpose and confidence down the hall. Everyone can see my self-esteem rising.

"Steve, don't worry if you don't get back to 100%. You should just be happy you are alive. That was a horrific accident you were in."

My blood boiled every time I heard that. I got so mad when the nurses and therapists would say that, because all I wanted was to return to 100%. I knew I was going to get back to 100%. There was not a doubt in my mind.

I firmly point at the nurses and say, "You're right, I'm not going to be 100%. I am going to be better than 100%!"

"Well, you know, one in a million make it back to being 100%." they reply.

"I'm the ONE! I AM THE ONE!" I point to my chest with conviction.

I am not sure why everyone at the hospital insists I will not return to 100%. Could it be they were trying to prevent me from going into a depression when I don't reach 100%? I am sure they have seen thousands of cases. But they have never seen me. On the other hand, maybe the nurses were trying to keep me internally motivated? It didn't matter what they thought. I was more determined than they knew!

Enlightenment

I ask everyone who comes to visit, "Home, home?" I can't speak in full sentences yet and am lucky if I even say the correct word. I have no expression and my voice lacks intonation. Everyone tells me the same thing:

"You can't go home yet."

I even ask my brother, who would visit me quite frequently. He calls me "Killer", which was a good boost to my ego. I always pictured a "Killer" as a tough guy on a hockey team. I know I look the complete opposite of a "Killer" but it felt really nice to be seen as a tough guy as he essentially was calling me a tough guy. But even he said, "Are you trying to trick me?"

My dad came by for a visit and I ask, "Home, home?" with my monotone, emotionless voice. He answers me with something different.

"When you get stronger."

It was exactly what I needed to hear. Why he said this, I don't know. I even think he doesn't know why he said it. But, once again, a switch in my brain flicked on. I know how to get stronger. That is something I can control. From now on, I will dedicate my hospital stay to physiotherapy and exercise.

Physio Determination Begins

One foot in front of the other. What a mystery it is for me to walk again. I am having the worst time trying to figure out how to walk. I can't seem to make my muscles coordinate to work to operate my legs. Here I am, standing between the parallel bars staring down at my feet. I have oversized shoes on because my parents had bought me some cheap runners they thought would fit. They were pristine looking, white high-tops: not anything special but they were mine. I was not allowed to have shoes for a long time, so any type of shoes was a treat. They were like skis.

"Your feet are so big!" a young, good-looking therapist comments. A good laugh ensues. (We all know what that really means.) I stand up even straighter.

It is the strangest feeling, not moving my feet. I just stare down at my shoes waiting for something to happen. Why are my feet not walking?

"Let's try again tomorrow, Steve," as my Physiotherapist walks over. I was quite perplexed.

Over the next month, I learned to move my legs again. I would go back to my room and practice moving my legs. Whenever I could not figure out a skill at therapy, I would go back to my room and practice my darndest to figure it out. If I could persevere through conquering one disability then I could conquer the others.

One day, out of the blue, I told my physiotherapist, "I used to be able to do one hundred push-ups. "

"I bet you can't do ten now." She sarcastically replied back to me. Challenge accepted!

I dropped to the floor and began to do pushups. There I was, nothing but skin and bone, doing push-ups. I struggled to do three and I can feel the strain on my muscles. Did I make a mistake? No way! Of course, I want to do the proper push-ups and touch my chest to the floor. None of those wimpy push-ups. I strive to do ten. I so badly want to prove her wrong. My pace is really slow now but I keep going. I manage to push myself to do another ten. I just did twenty push-ups. I was tired and sore, but I did it!

"You're going to prove me wrong every time, aren't you?"

"Yes, I am," I smile, very sure of myself.

My brain is starting to heal at an incredible rate thanks to all the effort I am putting into therapy, especially the physiotherapy. However, there is one disability that is still troubling me. No matter how hard I try and how many exercises I practice with my eyes, I can't get them to work properly. I only see out of one eye and the vision in that eye is blurry. To make matters worse, I cannot move my eyeballs downward.

I was at occupational therapy one day. They had given me the choice of two puzzles and asked, "Which one do you want to do?"

I answered, "The hardest one."

"I thought you might say that."

The occupational therapist gave me the harder puzzle. I completed the puzzle with little difficulty. I handed the sheet back to the therapist and said, "Done." I felt proud of myself for completing the harder puzzle. I wanted to continue proving the naysayers wrong and I wanted to go home as quickly as possible. She had a funny look on her face and said, "What about all of these?" I had somehow missed the entire bottom half of the page.

I was almost in tears. How could I miss all of those questions? I didn't show how upset I was because I wanted to seem strong. I took the page back and noticed I had only done half the work. I placed the page back into the exact same spot it was previously and then I noticed I couldn't see downward. I had to move my entire head to see below straight ahead. This would take some getting used to.

After occupational therapy, I had recreational therapy. There was not much time between therapy sessions. I was kept busy the entire day, going from one therapy to another. During recreational therapy, we would go for walks. It was usually myself, the therapist, and another patient. The other patient was usually another individual who was learning to walk again, just like me. The hospital grounds at Parkwood hospital stretched on forever. They were massive.

We started out on the walk and made small talk. I was bored and out of the blue said, "Can I run?"

"Were you a runner before?"

I told a small lie and said, "Yep."

"Ok then, run to the end of the edge of the grounds about a kilometre away. We will be behind these buildings still walking if you can't find us."

I proceeded to run. I remember beginning to tire fairly quickly. That was possibly because I had started out too fast. I didn't want to stop and take a breath or even walk because I wanted to prove something to this therapist. I ran and ran and ran. I arrived at the end of the compound and turned around. Sure enough, I came upon the two of them behind the building. I sprinted the last 100 metres because I wanted to prove I that I could do it and show the recreational therapist how easy it was for me.

My head was starting to pound. That was ok, as long as I didn't show it or admit to the pain in my brain. But a funny thing started happening. On my next run, I could go even further without my brain hurting. The pounding of my brain was becoming more bearable. The pounding only lasted a short time.

Through exercise, I was gaining confidence and a swagger. The therapists and nurses could witness the improvement.

"Don't worry if you don't get back to 100%."They would insist.

"You're right, I will be better than 100%!"

The Great Race

My physiotherapist seemed to be in on the conspiracy as well. She could also see that my confidence was increasing and I think that she was tired of hearing me say, "I will be better than 100%."

She decided to set up a running race. We went outside on a grassy area. She set up two sets of five cones in a straight line, 10 feet away from each other. We were both at our first cones. I had just learned to walk and run again but I thought I was a fast runner at this time.

She said to me, "If you win, you can go home."

My eyeballs lit up. She explained the race started at the first cone, run to the second cone, touch the ground, run back to the first, touch the ground, then go to the third and so on until you run through the fourth cone. I was extremely confident because I used to be a fast runner and I had been jogging a lot. I thought, *I will be going home in about five minutes after I smoke her in this race*!

She said, "Before we start, I have to warn you, I was on the national team for hurdles! On your mark. Get set. Go!"

We were both sprinting. We were neck and neck at the first cone. When we touched the second cone, she is slightly ahead. No worries, I will catch up. I am only playing.

All of a sudden, she starts to try. She accelerates at an insane speed. She sprints through the course to the end cone. Meanwhile, I am still at the second cone. *That's embarrassing*, I thought. *Oh well, it is another challenge to defeat. I guess I won't be going home any time soon. She was so fast it was like I was standing still. I probably was.*

"We will have to race again. Just give me a couple of weeks," I propose.

A couple of days after the initial race, I returned to my house in Chatham for a home visit. The race was still in the back of my mind. Behind my parents' house there is a large open field. I set up a course back there, the same way as my physiotherapist had set up her course. I practiced and practiced. Nothing was going to stop me.

After the weekend visit to my parents' house, I was back in the hospital. Within a week, my physiotherapist wanted to challenge me again. She was confident. I was confident. She set the cones up.

"I am going to beat you this time." I said.

"I don't think so, remember what happened last time?"

The race begins. The first cone we touch, we are neck and neck. At the second cone, we are neck and neck. Third cone, I start to pull ahead or at least I think I have.

She must be right on my rear. She is just playing with me. Sprint. Sprint. Sprint. Don't look back. She must be playing with me. I can feel her. She is right there. She will pass me at the end. Last cone. Touch. Where is she? I don't see her. Run. Keep running. Almost at the final cone. Sprint. Give it everything you've got. Keep going. Where is she?

I run through the final cone. My two arms up. I think I have won. I turn around. Where is she? She is way back there.

"I won!" I yell. "Can I go home now?"

"No. I never thought you would beat me!"

"Good enough." I said. "Just knowing I beat you is reward enough."

The countdown was on! A week went by and I was told the date I was going home. I marked the date in my calendar: 'Get out of JAIL.' I had stuck up a calendar on the wall to keep track of the days. Finally, I would be going home. Now what did life have in store for me? I am sure it would be another challenge.

On the last day of my lengthy hospital stay, the final therapist I saw before my discharge said to me, "So, you're ONE?"

I smiled and said "Yep."

After the Hospital

After leaving the hospital and rehabilitation services from Parkwood hospital, there was nowhere for me to go to continue staying in shape and physically fit. There were no more programs for me to follow and I could feel my body start to deteriorate and lose muscle and strength. My parents didn't want me to leave the house to do anything that might endanger me again. I found it very boring being home by myself while everyone was at work. I needed to do something but I couldn't drive anymore. I was like a prisoner in my own house. My fiancé was working during the day and I needed to keep my determination alive. I needed to exercise. I needed to challenge myself and succeed. Life was different now that I was out of the hospital. There was no more therapy, no more people telling me what to do. There was nothing, but I knew I needed something. I told my mom and she wanted me to be cautious. I understood her concern, but a life of languishing at home was not for me. But I really didn't know what I could do to help keep me on the road to recovery. So I researched exercise methods and did my best on my own to keep up the gains and progress that I had already made. It was difficult and not without a lot of frustration. But I was determined I was going to get back to 100%. I believed I could do it, and time would show that I could achieve it!

No One Will Hire a Guy Like Me

You've read about my determination to be 100% again, or to even surpass the health and abilities I had before the accident. I had a strong mindset to tackle the odds stacked against me, but it wasn't always easy. People didn't see me the same way anymore.

I look different and talk differently than other people. Who is going to hire a person that looks like me? People often didn't know how to relate to me. Some were unintentionally inconsiderate. Some were rather cruel.

"How can the public take a person like you seriously?"
"I can't even look at you."
"I don't know if you are looking at me or over my shoulder."
"You look and sound like you need a special school."
"You sound like you don't know what you are talking about."
"My dad said I don't have to listen to you."
"You don't need a mask for Halloween."
"You were not right for the job."

"Our volleyball game is being referreed by the one-eye wonder."

Those are just some of the unkind phrases directed toward me in the past.

My observation has been that if myself and another person walk into a job interview, with me looking as I do, scary and different, it didn't matter that I had similar credentials and better people skills and experience. I never seemed to get hired. First impressions mean a lot.

There have been many times when I have had an interview for a job. I get my hopes up that there is always a chance this could be the job for me. The interview seems to go well but then, I don't get the job. I have even had times when the interviewer said to someone that I was the best interviewee they have ever seen, but there was something about me they didn't like. I have spoken to someone that gave me a job because she was desperate. It was a type of job that only required a few hours a week. She told me as soon as she saw me, "Well, you were not exactly what I had in mind." I somehow managed to talk myself into the job. I pulled at her heartstrings with my story, and she felt sorry for me.

When I was an educational assistant for a while, I had by far more education and knowledge than many of the others and more than some of the teachers, but somehow, I did not get a full-time position. One look at me by parents and they are going to wonder why a disabled person is teaching their kid. I have felt the discrimination. I can't believe the type of people that are hired instead of me. I decided, if I can't get hired by someone else, I will create my own employment. Nothing will stop me from success.

Adults are shocked at times when they first meet me.

"Oh my god, what happened to your eye?"

"What's wrong with your voice?"

I question myself, should I wear sunglasses all the time? What would you do? Believe it or not, I have tried to wear sunglasses in public and I get phrases like, "You look weird with sunglasses on." I suppose I would look blind more than anything if I wore sunglasses all day.

I have felt the sting of discrimination. I have felt like I wanted to give up many times, but giving up would not solve anything. What will giving up accomplish? Instead, I have sought to prove them all wrong and become a success, in spite of it all!

Shortly after being married, I was running out of money, fast. I had a baby on the way. What was I going to do? I needed money to survive and could not find a job despite my best efforts. What was I going to do? I was getting down to my last dollar. It seemed that my only option was to apply for welfare.

I went down to the municipal office where the welfare office is located. I saw all different types of people waiting there. Most of those were dressed in ragged clothes and seemed not too pleased to be there. The smell of dirty people, booze and desperation hung in the air. I had never been around people like this sort before. It was something I was not accustomed to. So many people who seemed down on their luck, most likely due to their life choices. And there I waited and waited, trying not to make eye contact with anyone. I didn't want to be included in this group. I was feeling out of place, to put it mildly.

My insecurities got the best of me and I backed out of the line because they were taking such a long time and the lineup was ridiculously long. I was sure I could do better for myself, and I left with that thought firm in my mind.

Home Life

My university studies had been unfortunately interrupted. I needed to complete my degree and graduate. I only needed another 4 credits to graduate. In Chatham at the time, the University of Windsor was offering some courses. I said, "I don't care what courses they are. I will take them."

I took some psychology courses and as well as some communication courses. I had never taken communication studies before, but it turned out to be the most amazing course I had ever taken. The professor was my favourite and I learned a lot. I finished the class by getting the highest mark. The only way I remembered subjects was recording the professor's lecture on a digital device and writing notes at the same time. Each day when I got home, I would listen to the lecture over and over and fill in any notes and points I had missed the first time around. I had determination in my academic life as well. Life had a meaning to me. I was not going to give up on anything. Heck, I have conquered death, I can conquer anything life can throw at me!

Finishing my university degree was a goal I set for myself. What should have taken half a year to finish, took me 2 years. But I did it! I had to drop out of some courses and I failed others. But I stuck with it. I did not let anything hold me back. I did not want to give up on something I that had meant a lot to me. It was a firm goal I had set for myself. It would have been easy to quit. No one would have blamed me for leaving school but I had a drive and determination to achieve the impossible.

I eventually went back to playing soccer. At first, I had the most difficult time kicking a soccer ball. I had no muscle and had to relearn the kicking technique. Once I learned (ten years after my accident) I went back to playing an actual soccer game. It was strange playing with vision difficulty but I eventually learned how to play again. All I wanted to do was become a steady player again and to score a goal. I used to score a lot of goals when I was younger. I finally scored and then, I wanted to score even more! I was a steady goal scorer now but now I wanted to do something that was extremely difficult for anyone. I wanted to score a hat trick, three goals in one game! I kept at it. One game, every shot I took seemed to go in the net. Then it happened, I scored a hat-trick. Yes!

My dream of becoming a professional athlete was derailed for the moment. There was however another avenue I could still follow and reach success in sports, and that was through the Para national sports. It would take some adjusting but I decided to play for the Para national soccer team. For a couple years, I was involved with the Para national soccer team, travelling and living the life of an athlete. I believed in myself and achieved another life goal.

Back in Chatham, I was a member at one of the fitness clubs. I attended many aerobic classes and thought it would be amazing to be a fitness aerobics instructor and personal trainer. It would be even better to teach and coach physical fitness to those with special needs. I wanted to work with Dr. Svec to assist him and share my knowledge with him. He understood what I had been through and knew my expertise was valuable and we teamed up on an amazing program. Together, we developed Exercise MD.

ANYONE CAN HAVE THE EXTRAORDINARY LIFE. You have all the tools within yourself to become what you have always wanted.
BE THE ONE.

A Scary Moment

I was happy with the way my life and comeback were going. I had started to play soccer again. A sport I really enjoyed and was enjoying playing, even if it was the men's recreational league. It was great to feel the camaraderie again. By my fifth year of playing in the men's recreational league, I was starting to get into soccer fitness again and all seemed well. Each year I seemed to be on my brother's team. That always felt nice.

Games came and went each week. There were the usual tough battles and injuries to deal with but I was enjoying it immensely. My skills were improving and again I was one of the better players. One game, however, changed everything.

It was around the fifth game of the season. I jumped straight up for a head ball. It was around the midfield area of the field, nothing special, when out of nowhere a bigger player from the opposing team went up for the head ball against me. His shoulder slammed into my temple on the left side of my head. I blacked out. I went straight down; my body went limp. When my mind cleared again, I was laying on the ground on my side with one arm raised in the air. Everything went silent. I looked straight up to the skies and thought, *Oh no! Not again!* The referee blew his whistle to stop the game because he could see that I was injured.

I cautiously stood up. My right leg began to give way and I could see two players starting to make their way toward me to help. I took another step and my left knee started to collapse as well. The worst thoughts went through my head, *was I going to walk normally again? Had my brain been damaged seriously for the last time*?

The doctors had warned me about playing sports and that the next blow to the head could be fatal. I looked down the field at my brother who had a concerned look on his face. I could tell that he was worried. All that hard work I had put into rehabilitation, undone with an accidental blow to my fragile head.

What happened to all my strength? Why couldn't I stand up properly? What was happening?

It took a minute before I could figure out how to take a step with my other foot. My brain finally cleared and I was able to walk normally. I walked off the field under my own power and substituted myself. I only played a few more games and finished up the season.

That experience scared me a little too much and I retired from soccer after that season. I did not want to take any more chances. I realized that playing a sport was not worth injuring or even killing myself.

Re-Entering Society

I had worked so hard to get rehabilitated and get back to my old life, but things just weren't the same as they used to be, as I found out. People can be cruel to those whom they perceive as different from them. Here are two examples of my difficulties re-entering society.

Most days, when my fiancé finished her shift at the flower shop, usually around six o'clock in the evening, my parents would drive me over to her house. My driver's license had been suspended because of the injuries I had sustained during the car accident. We would quite often go out on a date.

One day, we had decided to go to a giant arcade. Each one of us was playing our own game. I was playing a motorcycle game that actually looked and felt like a real motorcycle. Cat was across the room playing a different game. I was alone for the first time. When my game was over, I started to climb off the motorcycle seat and for some reason, I could not lift my leg over the seat. So, I decided to step backward off the motorcycle but there happened to be a large block behind the motorcycle and I almost tripped and fell on my face. A young teenager was standing nearby with a group of his friends and sarcastically said, "Be careful, that's not like your motorcycle at home," and the entire group started laughing. I was completely humiliated. It seemed I was an easy target. What was I going to do? I was proud of being independent at the start of the day but that quickly turned into a lesson in humiliation. The struggle for acceptance back into the norms of society had begun.

Another time, my soon-to-be brother-in-law, Christian, wanted to go out to the badminton club and play badminton. I used to play a lot of badminton and was a pretty good player back in my high school days. Now I could barely see out of my right eye and my left eye was useless for vision as it was still stuck up and to the left. My shorts and shirts were oversized and about two sizes too big. I did not fit into my old clothes properly anymore.

We began playing badminton and rallying the birdie back and forth. I was lucky if I hit the birdie with my swing of the racquet. Christian wanted to challenge a couple of the young kids who were there. These kids were probably around fifteen. We started to play and somehow, we won the first game. I knew it was just luck that we were able to win. Those young, cocky boys were really mad now, and so they challenged us to another game.

I said to Christian, "Let's go. We shouldn't play." But he insisted. We started to play and I could tell that the boys were determined not to lose the second game. They started to show off, hitting us on purpose with their smashes and then laughing. They even played wrong-handed for a time period. The boys were laughing and joking, carrying on like they were the kings of the court. My eyes just couldn't focus that quickly on a small, fast-moving birdie. It was a blow to my ego, that's for sure. I swore that would never happen again. From that point on, I was more resolved than ever to get back to my old self, even if I couldn't see properly.

My fiancé continued to work at Stan's Flower shop and one time, I needed to see her at the shop. I was across town, close to her parents' house and thought it would be a great idea to borrow her father's bicycle. I did not even know if I knew how to ride a bike anymore. I borrowed his helmet that seemed to be a size too big for my head, so it slipped down over the top of my eyes. His bike was the old-fashion style of bike that seniors use. Here I was, wearing an extra-large helmet on my scrawny frame, wearing glasses and riding an old-fashioned bike. I was doing fine but as luck would have it, I rode past a couple of teenagers who cracked a joke about me. Gales of laughter ensued. Devastated, I knew that laughter was directed towards me. I turned around, returned the bike and helmet and then I walked to Stan's Flower shop.

It was a lesson learned. I needed to figure out how society worked and the intricacies of acceptance. I had never been such an outcast as I felt I was now. I was more determined than ever to be better than I was before the accident. My determination was now in acceleration mode.

Present Day

I look like I have just been through a war-zone, but I am still here. I am still alive. I am still persevering. Nothing will stop me from getting my message out there. Believe in yourself! You can achieve your dreams! I am very fortunate not only because I survived a severe accident but I am lucky enough to be able to speak again and share about what I have been through. I am also able to write. Not many people survive my experience and even fewer can speak afterward and fewer yet can write and string a coherent sentence together. You see, I wasn't supposed to survive. I will have a hole in my throat from the tracheostomy my entire life. The thought was that the doctors are not going to take all the trouble to sew the hole up when I am just going to die anyway. And why fix his eye when it won't be worth it to fix? He is going to die anyway. But I am still here. Fighting! Believing in myself. Making a believer out of everyone. You can make others believe in you by believing in yourself! Believe and live an extraordinary life!

Now that I have survived and achieved my goals, what am I going to do with this experience and knowledge? How can I help many people with the knowledge that I have accumulated? I can teach others how to achieve what I have. I can inspire others to achieve their goals. What a great world it would be if we all started to achieve our goals, no matter how impossible they may seem. To achieve a goal, you need a goal in mind and then you must picture yourself achieving that goal, feel yourself achieving your goal. Every day, believe you have that goal. Trick your mind.

The only way to change your situation is to take action. You can talk about the change you want to make. We all know the talkers in the world. But until you take action, it doesn't mean anything. Don't blame others for your misfortune and the problems that arise. Learn new skills to solve the problems. Improve yourself to improve your situation. If you want more, learn more. Take the action needed to learn more. Don't just hope things are going to change. *You* change. Don't pray for fewer problems, pray for more skills. The more skills and knowledge that you have, the more valuable you become. The more you know, the more you will be paid.

The disappointments that I experienced, I saw as challenges to overcome and to persevere. To prove that I could defeat any obstacle. And to prove people wrong who said I couldn't do it. Life is all about how you look at situations. You have the power to allow events to affect you however you want.

Find your motivation. In order to succeed, you must go beyond yourself and find what motivates you. Find your WHY and remember that every day. For some people, it's money; for other people, it's to prove others wrong. For others, to be famous. For others, to be an inventor or to improve life for humans. Anyone can achieve their dream. Find your purpose and achieve it.

The secret to being a stable topper in life is to find a way to serve many. It is the key to greatness and respect. Believe in yourself. Find your purpose. Teach for a higher purpose. Go beyond yourself. Live the extraordinary life!

Simple Lessons I Have Learned from Achieving My Goals

1. Believe you can achieve your goal. Don't let anyone put doubt into your mind. If people doubt you, no matter who they are, don't listen. Always have your goal in your mind; tell yourself every day that you will achieve. The subconscious is stronger than the conscious mind.
2. Never give up on the pursuit of your goal. Be patient.
3. Every day is a new opportunity to succeed.
4. Take action. Don't just talk about what it is you are going to do. Successful people take action immediately. They don't think about the problems that could arise. They take action and deal with the problems as they come upon them. Be a leader. Take action.
5. We all have greatness within. You attract what you feel about yourself. Believe your goal is possible.
6. Get to know as many people as you can.
7. You attract what you give out.
8. Impact others.
9. How we react to situations will determine our next step, which will determine our outcome, which will

determine our life, which determines our destiny. You have the choice in how you see life.

10. Focus on what you want. Focus on what drives you. Don't focus on the negative or what you don't want.

11. Have a goal.

12. Exercise can be like magic. It cures, keeps you healthy, helps keep your mind clear, improves your memory, improves your overall life.

13. Short term goals lead to long term gains. Every day is a new opportunity to advance further to achieve a small goal. Don't think of the big picture. Every day or week have a goal, achieve that goal and celebrate.

14. From my time in the hospital and my experience in helping others, I realized that there is always somebody worse off.

When you look at me don't feel sorry for me because I look different or sound different. I still have a hole in my throat and my eye looks really strange, going up and to the left like I am looking back into my skull. I feel blessed that I am able to speak to others and give advice and inspiration. I feel like I am the luckiest person on the planet. I experienced what no one else will ever get to truly experience and I get to inspire others from my experience. I get to share my gift with you. If we all could learn how to share our own gifts with the world, what a better place this would be. Learn to share your gifts.

I overcame death and disability to be here today. I am nobody special. If I can do it, you can too. It is possible to achieve any goal that you have. How badly do you want to succeed? Believe in yourself. Believe and you can achieve.

I NEED TO ACHIEVE. Anything is possible. Your dream is possible. You can be whoever you want. Don't stop because you failed once or twice, or ten times. All those failures are learning experiences and a lesson of how not to do it next time. If you want to achieve a goal badly enough, you will find a way. BECOME A SUCCESS

When I look back at my life, it had been preparing me for this moment. Life takes you through troubled times. There are peaks and valleys. Each one of those peaks and valleys is a lesson. Greatness doesn't happen overnight. Those in the world that have achieved incredible success have been through incredible failure and let downs. Don't give up when things are down. Don't listen to others' opinions of you. Believe in yourself. Keep a strong mind set. Everything you have gone through is preparing you for something great.

Lessons I Learned from Facing Death

I started to rebuild my life from behind everyone else. I started with major disabilities, I look different and I speak differently. I didn't listen to the people who said it was impossible for me to succeed. I told them that they don't know me and that it might be impossible for them to succeed, but not for me. I had higher aspirations and expectations of myself. The key word in this sentence is *expectations*. I have the attitude that I will prove them wrong and amaze them with what I can accomplish. It is possible to live an extraordinary life no matter who you are. It's a simple mind shift. Believe in yourself and your ability and you are halfway there!

Life becomes what you make it. If you focus on the negative in life, you will certainly find everything that is negative. If you focus on the positive, then you will certainly search out everything that is positive. There are two different ways to live the same life. A positive life always exceeds your expectations and a negative one has you asking the question, "Why does this always happen to me?"

Put yourself around successful people and learn what they do. Let their actions and habits rub off on you. Pay attention to their ways.

The WILLPOWER of the subconscious is stronger than you think. The subconscious determines your WILL, which determines your desire, which determines the outcome. If you believe, you can achieve. You become what you think about. You are what you think you are. If you always think about being healthy and strong you will figure out a way to become healthy and strong. You can manifest what you think about yourself and about your future. If you believe that greatness is within your reach, then you will accomplish it. Your will and way of thinking determines your path in life and your lifestyle. You live your life from your belief system. You will not stop until you accomplish your manifestation. Your will and way of thinking is what determines your path in life and lifestyle you live. You live your life from your beliefs.

If you want something in life, you have to go after it with everything you have. You can't wait around for someone else to help you. That person is not coming. Ultimately, it comes down to you. See it. Visualize it. Be it. The first step to becoming successful is to visualize yourself with the goal that you want to achieve. Not only visualize it, but feel it. Your mind does not know the difference between what is real and what is imagination. Imagination and visualization are considered the sixth sense.

Have a persistent attitude. If something does not work out the first time, learn from it and try again. There is no such thing as a failure. Every failed attempt is an opportunity that takes you closer to the solution and closer to your goal. As a child, when learning to walk, you did not just give up after the first attempt. After falling on your face, you were persistent until you achieved the goal of walking. Every great inventor has been through the same process. They failed and failed and failed. But they never gave up. They kept trying until they figured out their invention.

Determination and a persistent mindset are keys to accomplishing your goal. A never-give-up attitude. There is always a way to accomplish your goal. If you think you have tried every type of solution and still there is no success, there must be one more way for you to discover. Great inventors are a good example of this way of thinking.

Even the smallest step forward is a step closer to reaching your goal. Take action. Don't just talk. Take action and right away! Don't just talk the talk, but walk the walk; you will set yourself apart from ninety percent of the population if you start to take action toward your goal today. We all know there are a lot of talkers out there. The trick is: let your actions do the talking for you.

Put the work in. This is nothing new. If you want to be a better athlete; you must practice every day. If you want to be a better reader, you must read every day. If you want to learn a second language, you must try to speak in that language every day. If you want to succeed in life, you have to practice your craft every day. You must practice the right way if you want to be great. The best athletes and the best academics practice or study every day. I promise that if you put the work in, you will get the rewards. Every day is a new day and you must put in the work consistently. The first day is always the hardest day. They have scientifically proven that the seven days after that first day are the hardest days. Make your practice a habit. Start your day by practicing your craft so you will feel you have accomplished something to start your day. Starting your day with a success will translate to the rest of the day. You will be inspired for the rest of the day. Once you learn that you can change anything with a bit of practice, you will use that same skill to change your entire life.

You are where you are in life because of the way you think. If you always blame others for your problems and do not take any responsibility on to yourself, you will never get anywhere. You will never accomplish your dreams.

Push yourself to your limits and beyond. You always have a little more in the tank to push yourself. Limits are set by people who could not push to the next level. Limits and records are meant to be broken. When you think you have attempted every way to accomplish your goal, there is always one more way you have not thought about. Find it!

Make yourself valuable. Learn what is needed and how you can attain that value. Once you have attained that value, find a unique skill that sets you apart from the competition. Convince others why you are needed in order for them to be successful. Demonstrate your skills that set you apart from the competition. Don't wish for fewer problems; instead, learn more skills.

Everything happens for a reason. Sometimes bad things happen to us. Things that we didn't plan that might set us back many years. That thing that happened to us, happened for a reason. I look at life in that we all have a purpose. There is always a good reason why things happen. It is to push us closer to our purpose, closer to our destiny. Everything might not work out the way we want, but it will always work out for the best. Greatness can come from a great mess.

The past is the past, so leave the past behind. Just because it did not work out for you before does not mean it will not work out for you now. Shift your mindset. Believe good things are in front of you. See the good in every day. Picture things working out for you. At the end of the day, write a list of all the good things that you saw and that happened to you today. Writing a list will start to change your mindset to the positive.

Stay on top of things and anticipate any dramatic changes that may occur. It is the boy scouts' motto, 'always be prepared'; don't allow surprises to throw your life off track. Things like a sudden layoff, death in the family, bills or creditors that may come knocking. If your financial life is in order, you will have less stress and more enjoyable life.

Exercise is a key element to developing your physical body for success. Exercise does not necessarily need to be working out with weights or exhausting yourself physically. It can be as simple as a walk or yoga in the morning, a snack on exercise. Start your day off right. Get your blood flowing, get more oxygen to your brain for clearer thoughts and a positive outlook. Exercise changes your thinking ability; it changes your psychology as well as your physiology. You will think more clearly, solve problems more effectively and feel better about yourself. You will become more confident with yourself and your own body. You will have revelations you have not had before. Morning exercise is practiced by the most successful people in the world because they know it works to help their mind, body, and soul. Learn from the best. If you want to be successful, copy the most successful.

Create a one year, five year, and ten-year plan. Know where you are going and how to get there; don't drift through life without any direction. If you have no direction you won't have anything to strive for or to accomplish. You will become part of someone else's plan. As Jim Rohn says, "If you don't design your own life plan, chances are you'll fall into someone else's plan. And guess what they have planned for you? Not much."

What's Your Problem? Energy Suckers

Watch out for these people. Not everyone has your best interests in mind. Be aware and lose people these types of people. No matter how much the insurance company said they were looking out for my best interest, they were never looking out for me. They were always out for their own best interests; they are a company like any other. It does not matter what company it is; no one wants to part with their own money. They, too, were trying to save money. At one point the insurance company that I was dependent on to live, (they supplied me with a big monthly cheque), determined that they were no longer going to give me money. I was unable to work a full-time job after being released from the hospital. I did have a casual job working with others who had experienced a brain injury. It did not give me much money. It was a holiday in Canada when the insurance company cut me off and my lawyer was also not working that day. What a coincidence. I was beside myself. After a long weekend, I managed to speak with my lawyer and she said the insurance company was just playing games. My benefits were reinstated and everything worked out. The point is that not everyone has your best interest in mind. Be aware of energy suckers.

Certain therapists, especially certain psychologists, thought they knew me better than I knew me. They thought they were so smart and tried to analyze my brain. The only thing they were neglecting was as my spirit. They neglected the strength of my spirit. Don't let so-called professionals dictate your life and tell you what you can and cannot do. Someone's opinion of you does not have to determine your value. Don't wait for someone to give you permission to achieve your goal. You are the only person that has to believe in yourself to make your dreams a reality. IF YOU BELIEVE, YOU CAN ACHIEVE.

Don't let others bring you down, always think positively. Sometimes those closest to you will be your worst critics. There are a lot of people in the world that have never lived their own dreams or accomplishments and feel that your dreams and goals are impossible because they could not achieve theirs. Don't associate with people who are energy suckers. You want to be around people that are positive people and learn from them. You want their positive successful lives to rub off on you.

How Do I Stay Positive Now?

I realize that life is short and I have to make the best of every moment, enjoying the time I have. Find enjoyment in the little things. Celebrate the smallest victory. My small victory for me was kicking a soccer ball. After I learned to kick a soccer ball again, it was kicking a soccer ball straight, then it was kicking a soccer ball further than five feet, then running with a soccer ball at my feet. Another victory was learning to string two words together when I first learned to speak again. Even just learning to take a step on my own or making the motion of twisting a key to unlock a door. For ninety-nine percent of the population, these tasks would seem simple, but for me coming out of a coma, it was extremely difficult. Some of your challenges or victories may be easy for other people but difficult for you, and vice versa. No two people are going to have the same life challenges. Each day presents a new set of challenges. Set up your life so you celebrate a small victory every day. What you celebrate will not be the same for another person and there is no need to announce your victories. It becomes an internal victory. Every day is a great day because for one, you woke up and two, you have the opportunity to do something great. *Today* is the day great things happen.

Your life is meant to be enjoyed. Don't get frustrated if you don't succeed the first time or the fiftieth time. Learn from your mistakes and take a different approach. Just whatever you do; don't give up. You want to be a winner, not a loser. You want to overcome obstacles. Once you give up on one of your goals, you set your mind into a state where it thinks that it is fine to give up on any of your goals. That can produce a downward spiral effect.

Always keep in the back of your mind what you want to accomplish. Don't change your beliefs, no matter what others tell you. Listen to others because maybe they do have something that could help you, but don't listen if they feel your goals are insignificant. No two people are the same and no two people will have the same goals. It is your life, so keep a strong mindset on your ultimate prize.

Yes, I have a crooked eyeball and a hole in my neck and I may sound different but I am still strong mentally. I have come incredibly far. I have not come this far to stop and give up. I won't quit until I get what I want. My expectations are high. There is no need to announce my own goals, they are mine alone. No two people will find value in the same things. Sure, I have setbacks but I don't see them as setbacks. I see my setbacks as lessons and then I try to reach my goal from a different angle. It means I am one step closer to finding a solution.

The only type of people that try to put me down are people that are weak mentally; people that are jealous and envious at what I have accomplished. They cannot accomplish what I have and that makes them jealous and mad. I just laugh at them and feel sorry for people like that.

No matter what the challenge or obstacle in my way, I will persevere and defeat it. If you have the mentality of victory, you are certainly going to find a victory because you will conquer. If you have the mentality of success, you will succeed. It is the law of attraction. You attract what you are projecting. I choose to project the mentality of a winner and a never quit attitude and in return, I am surrounded by others who have the same attitude. The same law is held true when attracting the opposite sex. You attract the person you want to be, and in turn they are attracted to you. It's all about your attitude.

William James of Harvard University put it this way, "Human beings can alter their lives by altering their attitudes of mind."

One thing I have learned; life is about how I perceive it. A positive mindset results in a positive life. A negative mindset results in a negative life. How do you want to live your life? You can shape the life you want by your attitude towards it.

Life is too short to dwell on negative events. What you focus on will determine the quality of your life. Change the way you think and you will change your life. Believe you can change your life.

I want to make a difference with the lessons I have learned from death and disability. I feel very fortunate because not only did I survive a horrific car accident, but I was also able to rehabilitate. Many would not have survived in the first place. Not only did I survive but now I have a chance to talk about the experience and to write about it. I was blessed with the knowledge of the circumstances surrounding my coma and rehabilitation and now, I can write about it and educate others from my experience. Great lessons can come from great tragedies.

I have overcome insurmountable odds to be here. If I can overcome and prosper in the face of death and disability, I can overcome anything. Learn from my experience and you, too, can overcome anything. I have an unquenchable need for success and a drive to prove everyone wrong; join me and we can achieve the impossible.

I don't allow people that are negative into my life. I don't hang around LOSERS, people that are not going anywhere in life, the type of people that don't have a drive for a better life, the bottom feeders or false toppers.

It is not what happens to us that determines our future or the circumstances that happen, the same events happen to everyone. It is how we react to the events. We must change ourselves. We must change how we see the circumstances.

Anyone can be successful and overcome anything. Believe in yourself and you can accomplish anything. Don't compare yourself to others. No two people have walked the same path in life. What is easy for you may be difficult for someone else. We all have our unique set of skills and experiences. One thing I enjoy doing is speaking to as many people and trying to inspire them through my story. Let me help you become successful. Make today the start of your new life. Don't postpone your best life. Make today the day you change everything.

Live your dream today.

About the Author

Steve is currently married and lives in Chatham, Ontario with his wife and four children. He is dedicated to inspiring as many people as possible with his message of overcoming. He travels to schools and organizations across the country as a motivational speaker. He is passionate about instilling a belief in yourself and demonstrating that anything is possible.

Steve is available for speaking engagements. For more information or to book Steve, you can contact him at scbottrill@gmail.com.

Manufactured by Amazon.ca
Bolton, ON

21576082R00072